Clarinet
Scales & Arpeggios and Sight-reading
from 2018
ABRSM Grades 1–5

Contents

First published in 2017 by ABRSM (Publishing) Ltd, a wholly owned subsidiary of ABRSM
© 2017 by The Associated Board of the Royal Schools of Music
Unauthorized photocopying is illegal

Music origination by Julia Bovee (Scales & Arpeggios) & Katie Johnston (Sight-reading)
Cover by Kate Benjamin & Andy Potts
Printed in England by Halstan & Co. Ltd, Amersham, Bucks., on materials from sustainable sources

Grade 1

SCALES

from memory
tongued *and* slurred

one octave ♩ = 50

F major

G major

A minor
natural

or

A minor
melodic

or

A minor
harmonic

ARPEGGIOS

from memory
tongued *and* slurred

one octave  = 72

F major

G major

A minor

Grade 2

SCALES

from memory
tongued *and* slurred

ARPEGGIOS

from memory
tongued *and* slurred

one octave  = 84

Bb major

D minor

to a twelfth ♪ = 84

F major

C major

A minor

Grade 3

SCALES

from memory
tongued *and* slurred

to a twelfth ♩ = 63

A major

D major

B minor melodic

or

B minor harmonic

D minor melodic

or

D minor harmonic

two octaves ♩ = 63

G major

B♭ major

G minor melodic

or

G minor harmonic

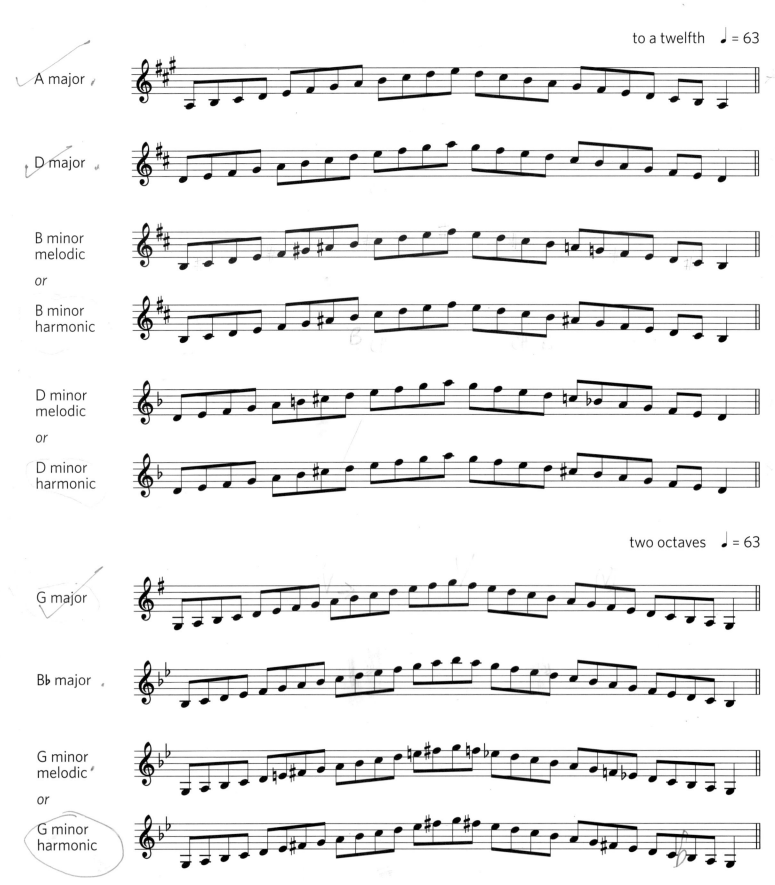

ARPEGGIOS

from memory
tongued *and* slurred

to a twelfth ♪ = 96

A major

D major

B minor

D minor

two octaves ♪ = 96

G major

B♭ major

G minor

CHROMATIC SCALE

from memory
tongued *and* slurred

one octave ♩ = 63

starting
on G

Grade 4

SCALES

from memory
tongued *and* slurred

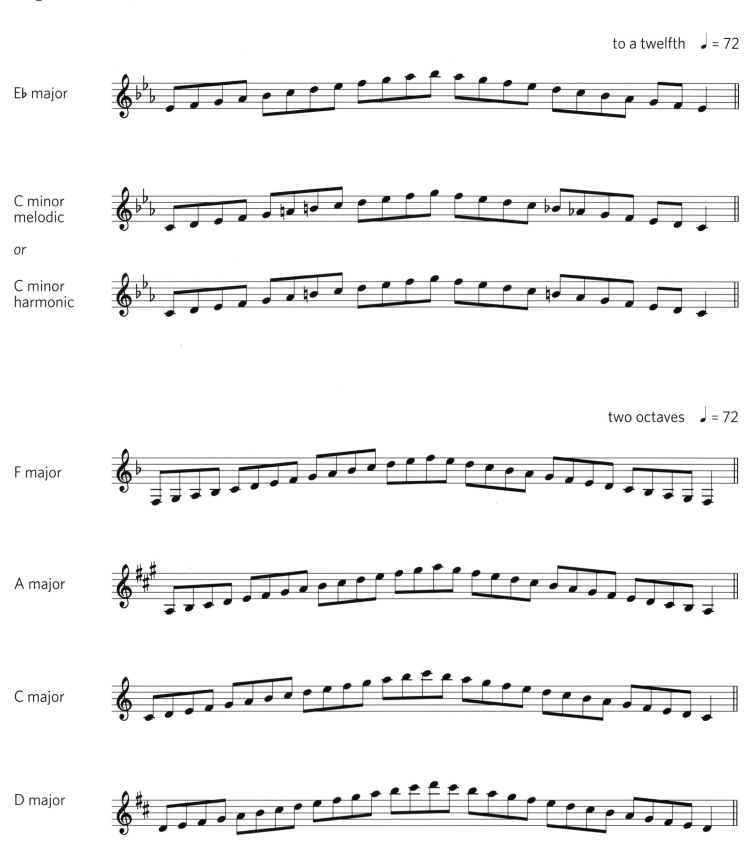

to a twelfth ♩ = 72

E♭ major

C minor
melodic

or

C minor
harmonic

two octaves ♩ = 72

F major

A major

C major

D major

A minor
melodic

or

A minor
harmonic

B minor
melodic

or

B minor
harmonic

D minor
melodic

or

D minor
harmonic

Grade 4

ARPEGGIOS

from memory
tongued *and* slurred

to a twelfth   ♪ = 108

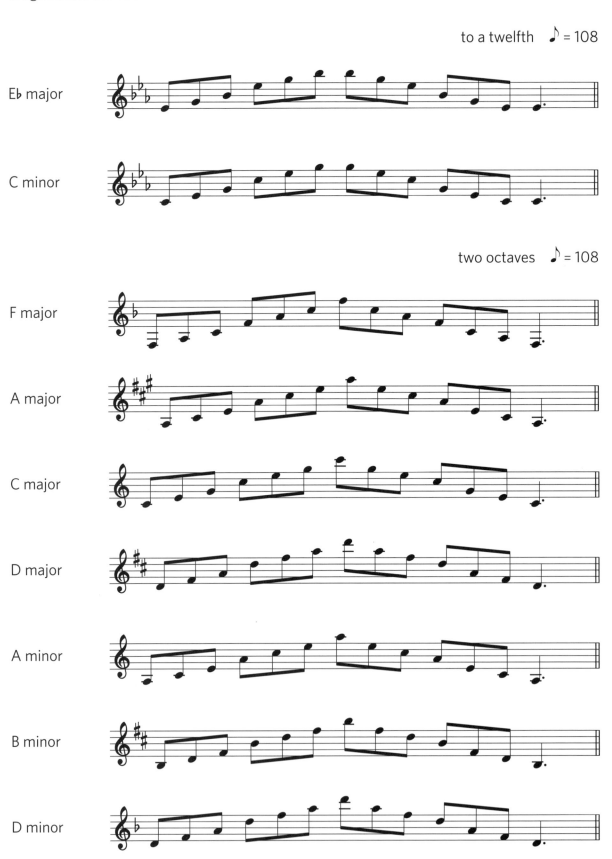

two octaves   ♪ = 108

Eb major

C minor

F major

A major

C major

D major

A minor

B minor

D minor

DOMINANT SEVENTH

from memory
resolving on the tonic
tongued *and* slurred

two octaves   ♩ = 54

in the
key of C

CHROMATIC SCALE

from memory
tongued *and* slurred

two octaves   ♩ = 72

starting
on F

Grade 5

SCALES

from memory
tongued *and* slurred

two octaves   ♩ = 84

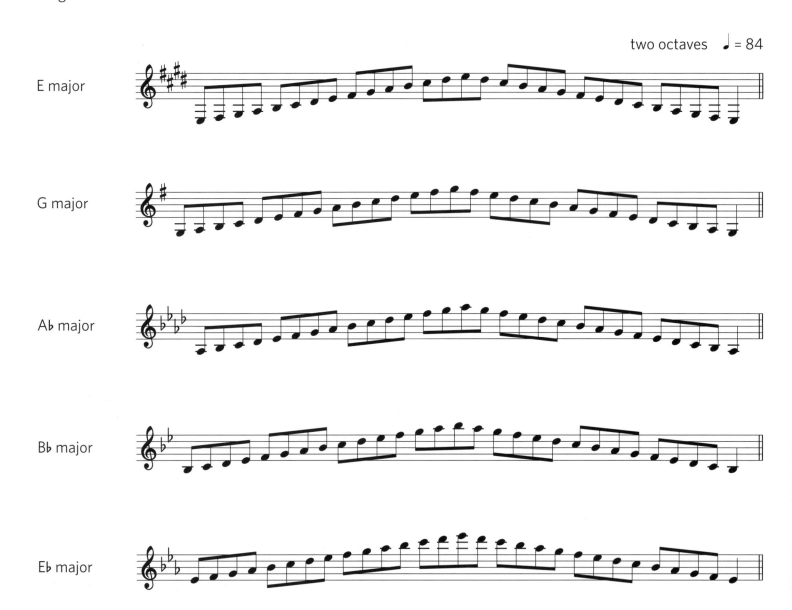

E major

G major

A♭ major

B♭ major

E♭ major

F minor
melodic

or

F minor
harmonic

F# minor
melodic

or

F# minor
harmonic

G minor
melodic

or

G minor
harmonic

C minor
melodic

or

C minor
harmonic

C# minor
melodic

or

C# minor
harmonic

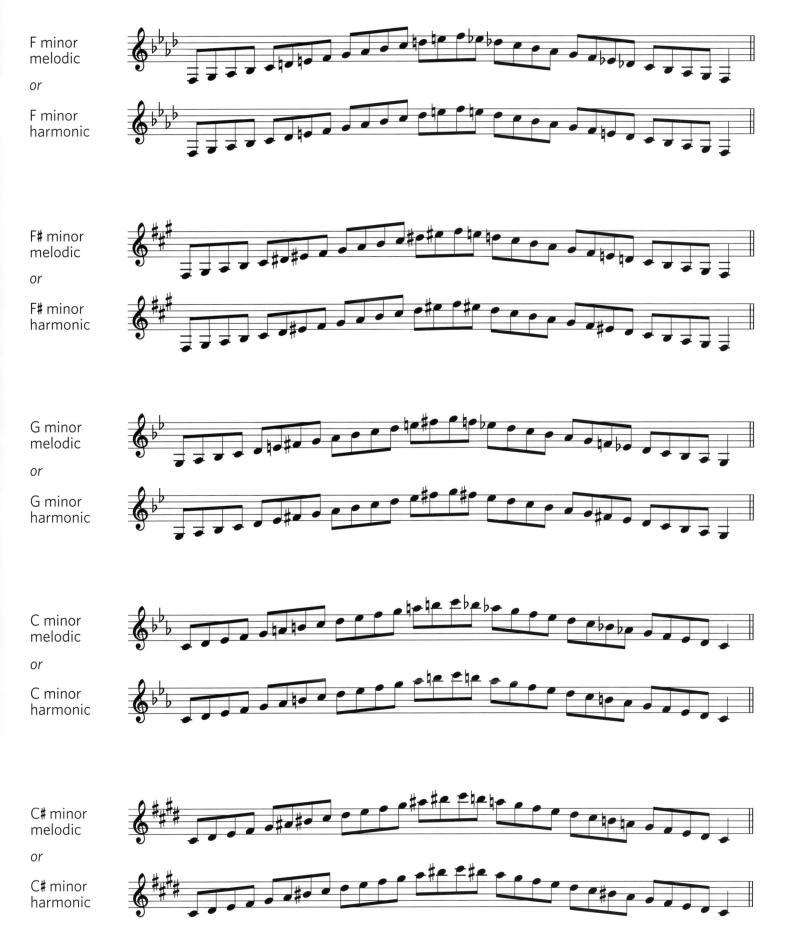

Grade 5

ARPEGGIOS

from memory
tongued *and* slurred

two octaves ♪ = 126

DOMINANT SEVENTHS

from memory
resolving on the tonic
tongued *and* slurred

two octaves   ♩ = 63

DIMINISHED SEVENTH

from memory
tongued *and* slurred

two octaves   ♩ = 63

For practical purposes, the diminished seventh is notated using some enharmonic equivalents.

CHROMATIC SCALES

from memory
tongued *and* slurred

two octaves   ♩ = 84

Grade 1 SIGHT-READING

Grade 1

Grade 2 SIGHT-READING

Grade 2

Grade 2

Grade 3 SIGHT-READING

Grade 3

Grade 3

Grade 4 SIGHT-READING

Grade 4

Grade 4

Grade 5 SIGHT-READING

Tempo di minuetto

1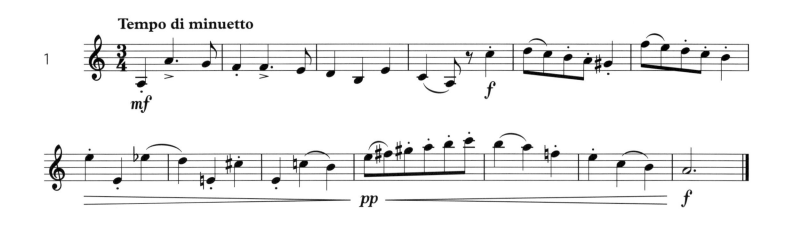

Allegro ritmico

2

Affettuoso

3

Grade 5

Grade 5

Grade 5

Misterioso

22

Scherzando

23

Marziale

24